ZERO TO TEN

For Sunny Jo, SS
For Keith and Fenny, SN

This edition published in 2003

Publisher: Anna McQuinn
Art Director: Tim Foster
Publishing Assistant: Vikram Parashar

First published in Great Britain in 2003 by Zero To Ten Limited
327 High Street, Slough, Berkshire, SL1 1TX

A CIP catalogue record for this book is available from
the British Library.

ISBN 1-84089-276-5

Printed in Hong Kong

Let's look at
MOUTHS

Written by
Simona Sideri

Illustrated by
Sheilagh Noble

This is my mouth.

Open wide and look inside.

Squirrels have big strong teeth and jaws.

Great for cracking open the nuts they love.

These gazelles have delicate lips – perfect for plucking acacia leaves without hurting themselves on the spiky thorns.

Butterflies have special mouths.

Excellent for
sucking up food.

Chameleons' tongues
are long and sticky.
They flick them out quickly.

Blink and you'll miss it!

Wild boars are hairy pigs.
They have hard snouts
for digging up roots.

The pelican drags its beak like a bucket
to scoop up fish - amazing!

My mouth is marvellous –
for talking and laughing,
munching and licking,
smiling and making faces!

Hardback
ISBN 1-84089-145-9

Paperback
ISBN 1-84089-273-0

Hardback
ISBN 1-84089-144-0

Paperback
ISBN 1-84089-274-9

Hardback
ISBN 1-84089-147-5

Paperback
ISBN 1-84089-276-5

Hardback
ISBN 1-84089-146-7

Paperback
ISBN 1-84089-275-7

"SEARCH FOR THE ROCKET"

ZERO TO TEN publishes quality picture books for children aged between zero and ten and we have lots more great books about animals! Our books are available from all good bookstores.

If you have any problems obtaining any title, or would like to receive information about our books, please contact the publishers:
ZERO TO TEN 327 High Street, Slough, Berkshire SL1 1TX Tel: 01753 578 499 Fax: 01753 578 488